I0426035

May 2012

SMALL EMPLOYER HEALTH TAX CREDIT

Factors Contributing to Low Use and Complexity

G A O
Accountability * Integrity * Reliability

GAO
Accountability * Integrity * Reliability

Highlights

Highlights of GAO-12-549, a report to congressional requesters

SMALL EMPLOYER HEALTH TAX CREDIT

Factors Contributing to Low Use and Complexity

Why GAO Did This Study

Many small employers do not offer health insurance. The Small Employer Health Insurance Tax Credit was established to help eligible small employers—businesses or tax-exempt entities—provide health insurance for employees. The base of the credit is premiums paid or the average premium for an employer's state if premiums paid were higher. In 2010, for small businesses, the credit was 35 percent of the base unless the business had more than 10 FTE employees or paid average annual wages over $25,000.

GAO was asked to examine (1) the extent to which the credit is claimed and any factors that limit claims, including how they can be addressed; (2) how fully IRS is ensuring that the credit is correctly claimed; and (3) what data are needed to evaluate the effects of the credit.

GAO compared IRS data on credit claims with estimates of eligible employers, interviewed various credit stakeholders and IRS officials as well as academicians on evaluation, compared IRS credit compliance documents with the rules and practices used for prior tax provisions and IRS strategic objectives, and reviewed literature and data.

What GAO Recommends

GAO recommends that IRS (1) improve instructions to examiners working on cases on the credit and (2) analyze results from examinations of credit claimants and use those results to identify and address any errors through alternative approaches. IRS agreed with GAO's recommendations.

View GAO-12-549. For more information, contact James R. White at (202) 512-9110 or whitej@gao.gov.

What GAO Found

Fewer small employers claimed the Small Employer Health Insurance Tax Credit in tax year 2010 than were estimated to be eligible. While 170,300 small employers claimed it, estimates of the eligible pool by government agencies and small business advocacy groups ranged from 1.4 million to 4 million. The cost of credits claimed was $468 million. Most claims were limited to partial rather than full percentage credits (35 percent for small businesses) because of the average wage or full-time equivalent (FTE) requirements. As shown in the figure, 28,100 employers claimed the full credit percentage. In addition, 30 percent of claims had the base premium limited by the state premium average.

Number of Small Employers Claiming the Full and Partial Credit Percentages, by FTE and Wage Requirements for the Credit, Tax Year 2010

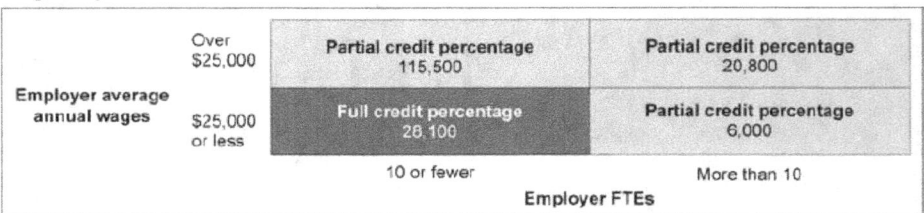

Source: GAO analysis of IRS data on Form 8941.

Notes: This information is based on the approximately 170,300 small employer claims. Numbers are rounded to the nearest hundred. Numbers don't add up because of rounding.

One factor limiting the credit's use is that most very small employers, 83 percent by one estimate, do not offer health insurance. According to employer representatives, tax preparers, and insurance brokers that GAO met with, the credit was not large enough to incentivize employers to begin offering insurance. Complex rules on FTEs and average wages also limited use. In addition, tax preparer groups GAO met with generally said the time needed to calculate the credit deterred claims. Options to address these factors, such as expanded eligibility requirements, have trade-offs, including less precise targeting of employers and higher costs to the Federal government.

The Internal Revenue Service (IRS) incorporated practices used successfully for prior tax provisions and from IRS strategic objectives into its compliance efforts for the credit. However, the instructions provided to its examiners (1) do not address the credit's eligibility requirements for employers with non-U.S. addresses and (2) have less detail for reviewing the eligibility of tax-exempt entities' health insurance plans compared to those for reviewing small business plans. These omissions may cause examiners to overlook or inconsistently treat possible noncompliance. Further, IRS does not systematically analyze examination results to understand the types of errors and whether examinations are the best way to correct each type. As a result, IRS is less able to ensure that resources target errors with the credit rather than compliant claimants.

Currently available data on health insurance that could be used to evaluate the effects of the credit do not match the credit's eligibility requirements, such as information to convert data on number of employees to FTEs. Additional data that would need to be collected depend on the questions policymakers would want answered and the costs of collecting such data.

_____ United States Government Accountability Office

Contents

Tables

Figures

Abbreviations

CBO	Congressional Budget Office
COBRA	Consolidated Omnibus Budget Reconciliation Act
FTE	full-time equivalent
HHS	Department of Health and Human Services
IRS	Internal Revenue Service
JCT	Joint Committee on Taxation
MEA	Math Error Authority
MEPS	Medical Expenditure Panel Survey
NFIB	National Federation of Independent Businesses
PPACA	Patient Protection and Affordable Care Act
SBA	Small Business Administration
SBM	Small Business Majority
SB/SE	Small Business and Self-Employed Division
TEGE	Tax Exempt and Government Entities Division
TETR	Telephone Excise Tax Refund
TIGTA	Treasury Inspector General for Tax Administration

United States Government Accountability Office
Washington, DC 20548

May 14, 2012

The Honorable Olympia J. Snowe
Ranking Member
Committee on Small Business and Entrepreneurship
United States Senate

The Honorable Sam Graves
Chairman
Committee on Small Business
House of Representatives

Many small employers do not offer health insurance to their employees. This is particularly true for small employers paying low wages. According to data from the Medical Expenditure Panel Survey (MEPS)[1] about 17 percent of employers with less than 10 employees who earn low wages (50 percent or more of their employees earn $11.50 per hour or less) offered health insurance to their employees in 2010, while about 90 percent of employers with 100 to 999 employees who earn low wages did.

To provide an incentive for small employers to provide health insurance, and to make insurance more affordable, Congress included the Small Employer Health Insurance Tax Credit (referred to in this report as the credit) in the Patient Protection and Affordable Care Act (PPACA).[2] The credit is available for tax years beginning after December 31, 2009 to certain employers with employees earning low wages— small business and tax-exempt entities—that pay at least half of their employees' health insurance premiums. The Congressional Budget Office (CBO) and the Joint Committee on Taxation (JCT) jointly estimated that the credit would

---

[1]MEPS is a set of large-scale surveys. MEPS is administered by the Agency for Healthcare Research and Quality in the Department of Health and Human Services. The 2010 Insurance Component survey had a response rate of about 83 percent for private establishments, and 38,409 respondents, including for-profit, and nonprofit employers; government units are excluded from these statistics.

[2]Pub. L. No. 111-148, §§ 1421, 10105, 124 Stat. 119 (Mar. 23, 2010), (codified at 26 U.S.C. § 45R).

GAO-12-549 Small Employer Health Tax Credit

cost $2 billion in fiscal year 2010 and $40 billion from fiscal years 2010 to 2019.[3]

You asked us to review the implementation of the credit. Specifically, we examined

- to what extent the credit is being claimed and what factors, if any, limit employer claims, and how these factors can be addressed;
- how fully the Internal Revenue Service (IRS) is ensuring that the credit is correctly claimed by eligible employers; and
- what data are needed to evaluate the effects of the credit.

To describe the extent to which the credit is being claimed, we reviewed IRS data on the claims for tax year 2010. To identify any factors that may limit credit claims and to assess how they could be addressed, we interviewed IRS officials as well as groups representing employers, tax preparers, and insurance brokers, and worked with them to assemble discussion groups on the credit. To assess how these factors could be addressed, we analyzed our interview results as well as relevant documents. Where possible, we identified IRS or MEPS data related to the factors. To assess how IRS is ensuring that the tax credit is correctly claimed by eligible employers we reviewed its compliance plans for the credit and compared them to practices used successfully for prior tax provisions[4] and IRS strategic objectives. We interviewed IRS officials on their compliance efforts. To assess what data would be needed to evaluate the effects of the credit, we conducted a literature review and interviewed interest groups and subject matter specialists from government, academia, research foundations and think tanks. We found the data we used to be sufficiently reliable for the purposes of our report.

We conducted this performance audit from July 2011 through May 2012 in accordance with generally accepted government auditing standards. Those standards require that we plan and perform the audit to obtain sufficient, appropriate evidence to provide a reasonable basis for our findings and conclusions based on our audit objectives. We believe that

---

[3]CBO, letter to the Honorable Nancy Pelosi, Speaker of the U.S. House of Representatives (Washington, D.C.: Mar. 18, 2010).

[4]For example, see GAO, *Tax Refunds: Enhanced Prerefund Compliance Checks Could Yield Significant Benefits*, GAO-11-691T (Washington, D.C.: May 25, 2011).

GAO-12-549 Small Employer Health Tax Credit

the evidence obtained provides a reasonable basis for our findings and conclusions based on our audit objectives. (See app. I for our scope and methodology.)

Background

Small Employer Health Insurance Market

Small employers with low-wage employees do not commonly offer health insurance, compared with large employers with low-wage employees, as shown in figure 1.

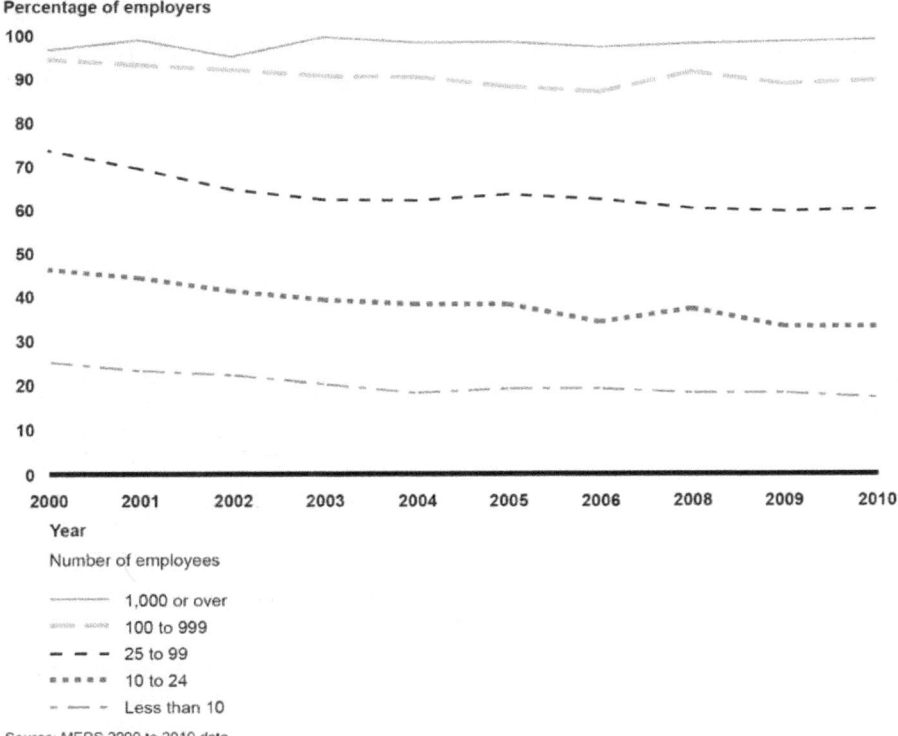

Figure 1: Percentage of Employers with Low-Wage Employees That Offer Health Insurance, 2000 through 2010, by Employer Size

Source: MEPS 2000 to 2010 data.

Notes: Figure includes for-profit and nonprofit (tax-exempt) entities but not government entities. A low-wage employer is defined as an employer that has 50 percent or more of its employees earning a low wage (earning $11.50 per hour or less, which is an annual salary of, at most, about $23,920). Data were not collected for the MEPS Insurance Component for 2007.

A combination of factors explains why small, low-wage employers tend not to offer health insurance.[5]

- For very low-wage employees, such as minimum wage employees,[6] health insurance drives up total compensation costs for employees.

- Low-wage employees working for small employers generally prefer to receive wages over insurance benefits as part of total compensation. On one hand, while employees pay both income and employment tax on wages, employees do not have to pay income or employment taxes on premiums paid by their employers for health insurance. However, for low-wage employees, the income tax exclusion is worth less relative to cash wages than for higher-income employees because low-wage employees may be in a lower income tax bracket.[7]

- Insurers of small employers face higher per-employee fixed costs for billing and marketing[8] and are less able to pool risk[9] across large numbers of employees. As a result, plans offered to small employers

---

[5]For additional description of challenges for small employers providing coverage, see GAO, *Private Health Insurance: Small Employers Continue to Face Challenges in Providing Coverage*, GAO-02-8 (Washington, D.C.: Oct. 31, 2001).

[6]In general, the federal minimum wage is $7.25 per hour. Many states also have minimum wage laws and minimum wages vary from state to state.

[7]See Quantria Strategies/Small Business Administration, *Health Insurance in the Small Business Market: Availability, Coverage, and the Effect of Tax Incentives* (Cheverly, Md.: September 2011).

[8]CBO estimated that for firms with 25 or fewer employees, 26 percent of premiums goes toward insurers' administration costs, compared with 7 percent for firms with at least 1,000 employees; see CBO, *Key Issues in Analyzing Major Health Insurance Proposals* (Washington, D.C.: December 2008).

[9]Risk pooling spreads risk across a group; a larger pool stabilizes the average insurance costs. Smaller risk pools raise costs because insurers run the risk of insuring those with relatively high health care needs. As a result, insurers may increase premiums to better ensure that they can cover unexpectedly large health care costs.

are likely to have higher premiums or have less coverage and higher out-of-pocket costs than plans offered to large employers.[10]

IRS Implementation and Requirements for Calculating and Claiming the Credit

IRS's Small Business and Self-Employed Division (SB/SE) and Tax Exempt and Government Entities Division (TEGE) are primarily responsible for implementing the credit. IRS works with the Department of Health and Human Services (HHS) and the Small Business Administration (SBA) on implementation tasks, such as outreach and communication.

To be eligible, an employer must:

- Be a small business[11] or tax-exempt employer[12] located in or having trade or business income in the United States and pay premiums for employee health insurance coverage issued in the United States.

- Employ fewer than 25 full-time-equivalent (FTE)[13] employees in the tax year (excluding certain employees, such as business owners and their family members).[14]

---

[10]The average deductible in 2010 per employee enrolled in a single (employee only) health insurance plan was $1,421 for employers with fewer than 10 employees; $1,420 for employers with 10 to 24 employees, $1,513 for employers with 25 to 99 employees, $1,155 for employers with 100 to 999 employees, and $738 for employers with 1,000 or more employees, according to MEPS. A deductible is the amount of expenses that must be paid out-of-pocket before an insurer will pay any expenses.

[11]For purposes of this credit, a business includes those that are corporations in a controlled group of corporations, or members of an affiliated service group, as well as partnerships, sole proprietorships, cooperatives and trusts. A sole proprietor is an individual who owns an unincorporated business but may employ others.

[12]The credit is available to tax-exempt employers described in 26 U.S.C. § 501(c) and exempt from tax under 26 U.S.C. § 501 (a).

[13]To calculate FTEs, the total hours of service must be determined for all individuals considered employees. There are a number of methods that can be used to determine the hours worked, but the hours are limited to 2,080 per employee. The total number of hours of service is divided by 2,080 to arrive at the FTE number.

[14]Other exclusions are seasonal employees, unless they work for the employer on more than 120 days in the tax year, and ministers who are deemed to be self-employed. Leased employees are included in FTE calculations.

- Pay average annual wages of less than $50,000 per FTE in the tax year.[15]

- Offer health insurance and pay at least 50 percent of the health insurance premium under a "qualifying arrangement." This means that the employer uniformly pays at least 50 percent of the cost of premiums for enrolled employees, although IRS did develop relaxed criteria for meeting this requirement for tax year 2010.[16]

The President's fiscal year 2013 budget request contains a proposal for expanding the credit's eligibility criteria to include employers with 50 or fewer FTEs and removing the uniform contribution requirement.

Limits on the Credit Amount

The amount of the credit that employers can claim depends on several factors. Through 2013, small businesses can receive up to 35 percent and tax-exempt entities can receive up to 25 percent of their base payments for employee health insurance premiums; these portions rise to 50 percent and 35 percent, respectively, starting in 2014. Employers can receive the full credit percentage if they have 10 or fewer FTEs and pay an average of $25,000 or less in annual wages; employers with 11 to 25 FTEs and average wages exceeding $25,000 up to $50,000 are eligible for a partial credit that "phases" out to zero percent of premium payments as the FTE and wage amounts rise. Figure 2 shows the phaseout of the credit for small businesses; the phaseout for tax-exempt entities follows a similar pattern, up to 25 percent of health insurance premiums.

---

[15]Wages for the employees included in the FTE calculations are included in average wage calculations except for minister's wages which are not subject to Social Security or Medicare tax.

[16]IRS offered a transition rule on the "qualifying arrangement" criteria for tax year 2010 and for satisfying the uniformity requirement. IRS Notice 2010-44.

GAO-12-549 Small Employer Health Tax Credit

Figure 2: Phaseout of the Credit for Small Businesses as a Percentage of Employer Contributions to Premiums, for 2010 to 2013

Number of FTEs	Average wage					
	$25,000 and less	$30,000	$35,000	$40,000	$45,000	$50,000
10 and fewer	35%	28%	21%	14%	7%	0%
11	33%	26%	19%	12%	5%	0%
12	30%	23%	16%	9%	2%	0%
13	28%	21%	14%	7%	0%	0%
14	26%	19%	12%	5%	0%	0%
15	23%	16%	9%	2%	0%	0%
16	21%	14%	7%	0%	0%	0%
17	19%	12%	5%	0%	0%	0%
18	16%	9%	2%	0%	0%	0%
19	14%	7%	0%	0%	0%	0%
20	12%	5%	0%	0%	0%	0%
21	9%	2%	0%	0%	0%	0%
22	7%	0%	0%	0%	0%	0%
23	5%	0%	0%	0%	0%	0%
24	2%	0%	0%	0%	0%	0%
25	0%	0%	0%	0%	0%	0%

Source: Congressional Research Service.

Note: GAO adapted the graphic from Congressional Research Service, *Summary of the Small Business Health Insurance Tax Credit Under PPACA (P.L. 111-148)* (Washington, D.C.: Apr. 5, 2010).

Further, the amount of the credit is limited if the premiums paid by an employer are more than the average premiums determined by HHS for the small group market in the state in which the employer offers insurance. The credit percentage is multiplied by the allowable premium to calculate the dollar amount of credit claimed. For example, in Alabama, the state average premium was $4,441 for a single employee in 2010. If an employer claiming the credit in Alabama paid $5,000 for a single employee's health premium, the credit would be calculated using the state average premium of $4,441 rather than the actual premium paid. Appendix II shows the average premiums by state.

The proposal in the President's Budget suggests beginning the phaseout at 21 FTEs, rather than 11, as well as providing for a more gradual combined phaseout for the credit percentages and removing the state market limits.

Process for Claiming the Credit

Employers are to calculate the credit amount on IRS Form 8941, "Credit for Small Employer Health Insurance Premiums." Small businesses are to claim the credit as part of the general business tax credit (on Form 3800), and use it to offset actual tax liability. If they do not have a federal tax liability, they cannot receive the credit as a refund but may carry the credit forward or back to offset tax liabilities for other years.[17] Credit amounts claimed by partnerships and S corporations are to be passed through to their partners and shareholders, respectively,[18] who may claim their portions of the credit on their individual income tax returns.[19] Tax-exempt entities are to claim the credit on Form 990-T, "Exempt Organization Business Income Tax Return," and receive the credit as a refund even though the employer has no taxable income.

Employers that claim the credit can also deduct health insurance expenses on their tax returns but must subtract the amount of the credit from the deduction. Employers can claim the credit for up to 6 years—the initial 4 years from 2010 through 2013 and any 2 consecutive years after 2013 if they buy insurance through the Small Business Health Option Programs, which are part of the insurance exchanges to be established under PPACA.[20]

---

[17]The unused credit for small businesses may be carried back 1 year or forward up to 20 years. Credits cannot be carried back to a year prior to the effective date of the credit; any unused credit amounts for 2010 can only be carried forward. See IRS Notice 2010-44.

[18]Owners of S corporations are referred to as shareholders. S corporations are corporations that "pass through" gains and losses to shareholders' individual tax returns without generally paying taxes at the entity level. Similarly, partners receive pass through income and losses from a partnership.

[19]For partners and shareholders, the credit is to be entered on the Schedule K-1 to be filed with an income tax return.

[20]PPACA requires the establishment of exchanges in each state by January 1, 2014, which are to help eligible individuals and small employers compare and select insurance coverage from among participating health plans. See Pub. L. No. 111-148, § 1311(b), 124 Stat. 119, 173 (Mar. 23, 2010).

Fewer Small Employers Claimed the Credit Than Were Thought to Be Eligible Because of Factors Such as Credit Size and Complexity

Actual Credit Claims Were Much Lower Than Initial Rough Eligibility Estimates

Fewer small employers claimed the credit for tax year 2010 than were thought to be eligible based on rough estimates of eligible employers made by government agencies and small business groups. IRS data on total claimants, adjusted to account for claims by partners and shareholders, show that about 170,300 small employers made claims for the credit in 2010.[21] (See app. III for adjustments to determine claims filed by employers.) The average credit amount claimed was about $2,700. Limited information is available on the distribution of claim amounts for business entities because IRS focuses its data collection on the taxpayers filing credit claims, who may be partners or shareholders claiming their portions of a business entity's credit. Appendix III provides additional detail.

Selected estimates, made by government agencies and small business groups, of employers eligible for the credit range from around 1.4 million to 4 million. However, data limitations mean that these estimates are necessarily rough. Based on our review of available data sources on the three basic eligibility rules for the credit—involving wages, FTEs, and health insurance—it is not possible to combine data from various sources to closely match these rules. (See app. VI for details.) Though statistical modeling corrects for imperfect data to match these rules, models are not precise. While acknowledging the data limitations, several entities produced estimates of the number of employers potentially eligible for the credit. The Council of Economic Advisors estimated 4 million and SBA

---

[21]The number of employees who had their premiums paid by employers that claimed the credit was about 770,000.

estimated 2.6 million.[22] Other groups making estimates included small business groups such as the Small Business Majority (SBM) and the National Federation of Independent Businesses (NFIB). Their estimates were 4 million and 1.4 million, respectively.[23]

A similar pattern is seen when the dollar value of credits actually claimed is compared to initial estimates. The dollar value of claims made in 2010 was $468 million compared to initial cost estimates of $2 billion for 2010 (a CBO and JCT joint estimate).[24]

Most Small Employer Claims Were Reduced Because of the Phaseout Rules and Some Were Reduced by the State Average Premiums

Most of the claims were for less than the full credit percentage. Of the approximately 170,300 small employers making claims for tax year 2010, 142,200—83 percent—could not use the full credit percentage. Usually employers could not meet the average wage requirement to claim the full percentage, as about 68 percent did not qualify based on wages but did meet the FTE requirement. (See fig. 3.)[25]

Credit Phaseout

(In reference to the phaseout) "People get excited that they're eligible and then they do the calculations and it's like the bottom just falls out of it and it's not really there. It's almost like a wish that they might get it and then they do the calculations and it's not worth it for them." –Health insurance discussion group participant

---

[22]The Council of Economic Advisors is an agency within the Executive Office of the President charged with offering objective advice on the formulation of domestic and international economic policy, and SBA is a government agency that offers a variety of programs and support services to help small businesses.

[23]The estimate for SBM and SBA included nonprofits. The estimate for NFIB was only for small businesses; it is not known whether the estimate for the Council of Economic Advisors included nonprofits in addition to businesses.

[24]CBO and JCT recently reduced their original estimates of the future costs of the credit to a cost of $1 billion in 2012 and a cost of $21 billion from 2012 to 2021. These estimates were previously $5 billion in 2012 and $40 billion from 2012 to 2021.

[25]See app. IV for a graph of claimants with fewer than 10 FTEs and the amount of full credits.

Figure 3: Percentage and Number of Small Employers Claiming the Full and Partial Credit Percentages, by FTE and Wage Requirements for the Credit, Tax Year 2010

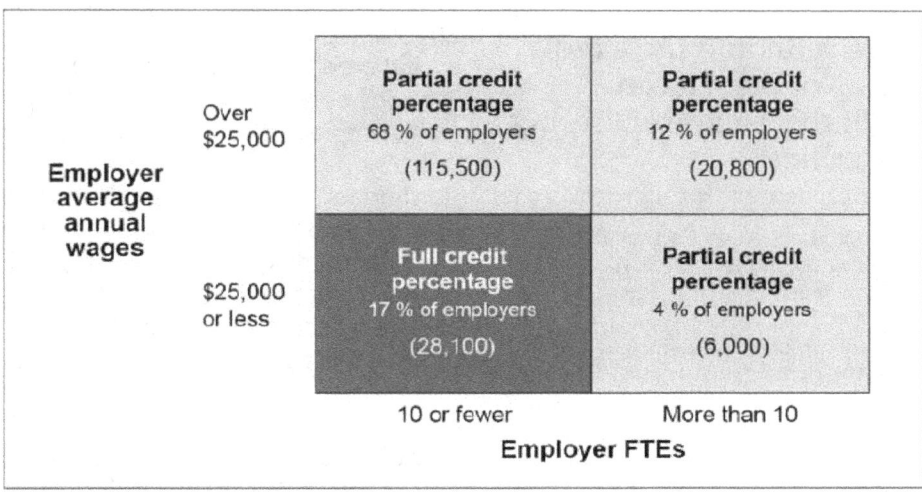

Source: GAO analysis of IRS data on Form 8941.

Notes: This information is based on the approximately 170,300 small employer claims. Numbers are rounded to the nearest hundred. Numbers and percentages do not add to totals because of rounding.

State average premiums also reduced some credit amounts by reducing the amount of the premium base against which the credit percentage is applied. This premium base may be reduced when it exceeds the state average premiums for small group plans,[26] as determined by HHS. If so, small employers are to use the state average amount, which in essence caps the premium amount used to calculate their credit. According to IRS data, this cap reduced the credit for around 30 percent of employer claims. For example, a nonprofit representative told us that her credit dropped from $7,900 to $3,070 because of the cap in her state. (See app. II for small group average premiums in all states.)

---

[26]A small group plan is a health coverage plan sponsored by small employers for the employees.

Most Small Employers Could Not Meet the Health Insurance Requirement for the Credit and the Credit Was Not Seen as an Incentive to Start Offering Insurance

As already discussed, small employers do not commonly offer health insurance. MEPS estimates that 83 percent of employers who may otherwise be eligible for the full credit[27] did not offer health insurance in 2010 and that 67 percent of employers who could be eligible for the partial credit[28] did not offer insurance. Our discussion groups and other interviewees confirmed this, with comments and examples of small, low-wage employers not offering health insurance to employees.

Small, Low-Wage Employers Not Commonly Offering Health Insurance

"Very few people are going to pay 50 or 100 percent of the health insurance for someone making $25,000 or less. We just don't have that many clients who even start to qualify." –Tax preparer discussion group participant

Furthermore, the small employers do not likely view the credit as a big enough incentive to begin offering health insurance and to make a credit claim, according to employer representatives, tax preparers, and insurance brokers we met with. While some small employers could be eligible for the credit if they began to offer health insurance, small business group representatives and discussion group participants told us that the credit may not offset costs enough to justify a new outlay for health insurance premiums. Related to this concern, the credit being available for 6 years overall and just 2 consecutive years after 2014 further detracts from any potential incentive to small employers to start offering health insurance in order to claim the credit.

Complexity Deterred Small Employer Claims, According to Discussion Groups

Most discussion group participants and groups we interviewed found the tax credit to be complicated, deterring small employers from claiming it. The complexity arises from the various eligibility requirements, the various data that must be recorded and collected, and number of worksheets to be completed.

Complexity of the Credit

"Any credit that needs a form that takes 25 lines and seven work sheets to build to those 25 lines is too complicated." –Tax preparer discussion group participant.

A major complaint we heard centered on gathering information for and calculating FTEs and the health insurance premiums associated with those FTEs. Eligible employers reportedly did not have the number of hours worked for each employee readily available to calculate FTEs and their associated average annual wages nor did they have the required health insurance information for each employee readily available.

---

[27]This MEPS statistic is based on employers—both profit and nonprofit—with fewer than 10 employees that pay annual wages of $24,000 or less to over half of their employees.

[28]This MEPS statistic is based on employers—both profit and nonprofit—with 10 to 25 employees that pay annual wages of $24,000 or less to over half of their employees. Because the employers eligible for the partial credit can pay up to $50,000 in wages, this is a less precise estimate than using MEPS to estimate insurance offerings for the full credit.

Exclusions from the definition of "employee" and other rules make the calculations complex. For example, seasonal employees are excluded from FTE counts but insurance premiums paid on their behalf count toward the employer's credit. Incorporating the phaseout also complicates the credit calculation.

In our discussion groups with tax preparers, we heard that small business owners generally do not want to spend the time or money to gather the necessary information to calculate the credit, given that the credit will likely be insubstantial. Tax preparers told us it could take their clients from 2 to 8 hours or possibly longer to gather the necessary information to calculate the credit and that the tax preparers spent, in general, 3 to 5 hours calculating the credit.[29] We did hear from a couple of participants— a small business owner and a nonprofit representative—that they did not find the credit overly burdensome.

Tax preparers we interviewed said that IRS did the best it could with the Form 8941 given the credit's complexity. IRS officials said they did not receive criticism about Form 8941 itself but did hear that the instructions and its seven worksheets were too long and cumbersome for some claimants and tax preparers. On its website, IRS tried to reduce the burden on taxpayers by offering "3 Simple Steps" as a screening tool to help taxpayers determine whether they might be eligible for the credit. However, to calculate the actual dollars that can be claimed, the three steps become 15 calculations, 11 of which are based on seven worksheets, some of which request multiple columns of information. Figure 4 aligns IRS's "3 Simple Steps," with the seven worksheets in the instructions for Form 8941 and the lines on Form 8941. (See app. V for full text for this figure.)

---

[29]The National Society of Accountants conducted a survey in 2008 that estimated the hourly tax preparer fee to be $122 an hour. Tax preparers may not necessarily charge for the credit, according to some discussion group participants.

GAO-12-549 Small Employer Health Tax Credit

Figure 4: Form 8941 and Credit Calculations on Worksheets Related to IRS's "3 Simple Steps" for Determining Potential Eligibility

Directions:

 Roll over the buttons below to reveal the worksheets necessary to calculate credit totals needed for lines on IRS Form 8941.

Step 1	Step 2	Step 3	
Determine the total number of employees (FTEs)	Determine the average annual wages paid to employees	Determine if you pay at least of half insurance premiums for employees	Additional calculations (FTE and wage phase out)

Form **8941**	Credit for Small Employer Health Insurance Premiums	OMB No. 1545-2198
Department of the Treasury Internal Revenue Service	▶ See separate instructions. ▶ Attach to your tax return.	20**10** Attachment Sequence No. **63**

Name(s) shown on return | Identifying number

1	Enter the number of individuals you employed during the tax year who are considered employees for purposes of this credit (see instructions)	1
2	Enter the number of full-time equivalent employees you had for the tax year (see instructions). If you entered 25 or more, skip lines 3 through 11 and enter -0- on line 12	2
3	Average annual wages you paid for the tax year (see instructions). If you entered $50,000 or more, skip lines 4 through 11 and enter -0- on line 12	3
4	Premiums you paid during the tax year for employees included on line 1 for health insurance coverage under a qualifying arrangement (see instructions)	4
5	Premiums you would have entered on line 4 if the total premium for each employee equaled the average premium for the small group market in which you offered health insurance coverage (see instructions)	5
6	Enter the **smaller** of line 4 or line 5	6
7	Multiply line 6 by the applicable percentage: • Tax-exempt small employers, multiply line 6 by 25% (.25) • All other small employers, multiply line 6 by 35% (.35)	7
8	If line 2 is 10 or less, enter the amount from line 7. Otherwise, see instructions	8
9	If line 3 is $25,000 or less, enter the amount from line 8. Otherwise, see instructions	9
10	Enter the total amount of any state premium subsidies paid and any state tax credits available to you for premiums included on line 4 (see instructions)	10
11	Subtract line 10 from line 4. If zero or less, enter -0-	11
12	Enter the **smaller** of line 9 or line 11	12
13	If line 12 is zero, skip lines 13 and 14 and go to line 15. Otherwise, enter the number of employees included on line 1 for whom you paid premiums during the tax year for health insurance coverage under a qualifying arrangement (see instructions)	13
14	Enter the number of full-time equivalent employees you would have entered on line 2 if you only included employees included on line 13	14
15	Credit for small employer health insurance premiums from partnerships, S corporations, cooperatives, estates, and trusts (see instructions)	15
16	Add lines 12 and 15. Partnerships and S corporations, stop here and report this amount on Schedule K; all others, go to line 17	16
17	Credit for small employer health insurance premiums included on line 16 from passive activities (see instructions)	17
18	Subtract line 17 from line 16	18

Source: GAO analysis of IRS information.

 **Print instructions** | To view and print full noninteractive versions of IRS Form 8941 and worksheets included in this graphic, go to appendix V.

Given the effort involved to make a claim and the uncertainty about the credit amounts, a few discussion group participants said it would be helpful to be able to quickly estimate employers' eligibility for the credit and the amount they might receive; this would help them to decide whether the credit would be worth the effort, although this would not reduce the complication of filing out Form 8941 because, to fill out the form, full documentation would need to be reviewed. IRS's Taxpayer Advocate Service[30] is developing a calculator for IRS's website to quickly estimate an employer's eligibility, but this will still require gathering information such as wages, FTEs, and insurance plans. We also heard concerns that a calculator could cause confusion for clients who find they are eligible when quickly estimating the credit but then turn out to be ineligible or find they are eligible for a smaller credit when their accountant fills out Form 8941.

The Extent to Which Lack of Awareness Is a Factor Limiting More Claims Is Unknown, Although IRS Did Significant Outreach

Many small businesses reported that they were unaware of the credit. The NFIB Research Foundation[31] and the Kaiser Family Foundation both estimated that approximately 50 percent of small businesses were aware of the credit, as of May 2011, or more than 1 year after Congress authorized this credit.[32]

The extent to which being unaware prevented eligible employers from claiming the credit for tax year 2010 is not known. Some discussion group participants raised concerns about unawareness, but they also cited other factors limiting credit claims for tax year 2010. If 50 percent of small businesses knew about the credit, then the approximately 170,300 claims is a relatively small proportion of those that were knowledgeable. This indicates that other factors contributed to employers not claiming the credit. Further, it is hard to interpret the impact of awareness on claims because these surveys included an unknown number of small business

---

[30]The Taxpayer Advocate Service is an independent organization within the IRS that helps taxpayers who are experiencing economic harm; are seeking help in resolving problems with IRS; and believe an IRS system or procedure is not working as it should.

[31]The NFIB Research Foundation is a nonprofit affiliated with NFIB.

[32]NFIB conducted this survey in April and May 2011 of 750 small employers of firms with 50 or fewer employees. The Kaiser Family Foundation conducted its survey from January through May 2011 of 3,184 public and private firms with 3 or more employees and its questions about the credit were directed to employers with 50 or fewer employees.

employers that would not be eligible for the credit regardless of their awareness. For those employers that were unaware, the surveys did not account for their accountants or tax preparers that may have known about the credit but did not tell their clients about it because they did not believe their clients would qualify or because the credit amount would be very small. In addition, the surveys did not cover tax-exempt entities.

To raise awareness of the credit, IRS did significant outreach. IRS developed a communication and outreach plan, written materials on the credit, a video, and a website. IRS officials also reached out to interest groups about the credit and developed a list of target audiences and presentation topics. IRS officials began speaking at events in April 2010 to discuss the credit and attended over 1,500 in-person or web-based events from April 2010 to February 2012. Discussion of the credit at the events varied from being a portion of a presentation covering many topics to some events that focused on the credit with a dedicated discussion period.

IRS does not know whether its outreach efforts actually increased awareness of the credit or were otherwise cost-effective. It would be challenging to estimate the impact of IRS's outreach efforts on awareness with a rigorous methodology; however, based on ongoing feedback they received from interest groups, IRS officials told us they believe their efforts have been worthwhile. IRS used some feedback from focus groups of tax preparers and from other sources[33] to revise its outreach efforts. For example, IRS modified its outreach from initially focusing on tax preparers and small employers to including insurance brokers in 2012.

Addressing Factors and Expanding Credit Use May Require Substantive Design Changes

Given that most small employers do not offer insurance and what we heard about the size of the credit not being big enough to incentivize offering health insurance,[34] it may not be possible to significantly expand credit use without changing the credit's eligibility. Most claims were for partial credits and many people we spoke with view the credit amount as

---

[33]Each focus group in 2011 consisted of 12 tax preparers. IRS issued a report on the focus groups' results on October 14, 2011.

[34]Given the previously discussed lack of knowledge or awareness, it is not clear that increasing outreach would increase credit usage.

too small and temporary to justify providing health insurance when none is provided now. In addition, given that IRS has conducted extensive outreach about the credit, it is not likely that more outreach would significantly increase the number of businesses claiming the credit. Amending the eligibility requirements or increasing the amount of the credit may allow more businesses to take advantage of the credit,[35] but these changes would increase its cost to the Federal government. Options include the following:

- Increasing the amount of the full credit, the partial credit, or both.
- Increasing the amount of the credit for some by eliminating state premium averages.
- Expanding eligibility requirements by increasing the number of FTEs and wage limit allowable for employers to claim the partial credit, the full credit, or both. This expansion would not, however, likely affect the smallest employers which do not offer health insurance.
- Simplifying the calculation of the credit in the following ways:
  - Using the number of employees and wage information already reported on the employer's tax return. This could reduce the amount of data gathering as well as credit calculations because eligibility would be based on the number of employees and not FTEs. A trade-off with this option would be less precision in targeting the full and partial credit amount to specific small employer subgroups.[36]
  - Offering a flat credit amount per FTE (or number of employees) rather than a percentage, which would reduce the precision in targeting the credit.

---

[35]Three bills were recently introduced to amend the small employer health insurance credit to increase the maximum number of FTEs to 50, modify the phase out of the credit amount, and repeal the limitation based on state health insurance premium averages. H.R. 4324, Small Business Employee Health Insurance Credit Expansion Act of 2012, also would repeal the 2-year limit after 2014, making the credit available indefinitely. H.R.4252 and S.2227, both titled Small Business Health Care Tax Credit Improvement Act of 2012, propose to increase allowable average annual salaries paid to employees to $28,500 to claim the full credit.

[36]Using the number of employees instead of FTEs would require an increase in the number of eligible employees in order to reach the same population of small employers. For example, two part-time employees working 20 hours per week count as one FTE, making the employer appear larger than if FTEs were counted.

The data limitations that made it difficult to estimate the number of businesses eligible for the current credit also make it difficult to estimate the impact of any design changes.

IRS Is Implementing Several Practices from Prior Compliance Efforts, but Additional Steps Could Be Taken

IRS Incorporated Practices from Strategic Objectives and Prior Compliance Efforts

IRS's compliance efforts for the credit incorporate practices that have been shown effective in helping to ensure compliance with other tax provisions or are consistent with IRS strategic objectives. Some of those practices were used for the Telephone Excise Tax Refund (TETR)[37] and Consolidated Omnibus Budget Reconciliation Act (COBRA) subsidies for health insurance for the unemployed, according to IRS officials.[38] Specifically, IRS is doing the following:

- Using computerized filters to review credit claims on Forms 8941 for certain errors or potential problems that may trigger an examination of the claim.

- Transcribing more lines of data from Form 8941 into IRS computer systems which should make the filters more effective. Although transcribing more lines increases processing and data storage costs, IRS plans to transcribe more lines for tax years 2011 and 2012 claims to ensure better verification of eligibility.

---

[37]We found that that IRS's compliance plans for the TETR were consistent with good management practices in previous reports. See GAO, *Tax Administration: Telephone Excise Tax Refund Requests Are Fewer Than Projected and Have Had Minimal Impact on IRS Services*, GAO-07-695 (Washington, D.C.: Apr. 11, 2007).

[38]We tested IRS's internal controls for the COBRA unemployment subsidies in the American Recovery and Reinvestment Act and found that IRS was able to identify all five fictitious companies used to fraudulently apply for the subsidies. See GAO *Proactive Testing of ARRA Tax Credits for COBRA Premium Payments*, GAO-10-804R (Washington, D.C.: June 14, 2010).

- Freezing refunds of tax-exempt entities whose returns have been selected for examination, which avoids the costs of trying to recover funds.[39]

- Considering the documentation burden on claimants. IRS did not require claimants to submit documentation on health insurance premiums with their Form 8941 because IRS officials said they will review examination results and may revisit the decision not to require documentation if results suggest that such documentation would improve compliance checks.

- Modifying filters, as needed, in response to observed trends. For example, a filter that applies to tax-exempt organization claims was tripped by about a quarter of claimant organizations, as of December 31, 2011. IRS officials said some eligible tax-exempt entities tripped the filter because it was too broad. To address this, IRS modified the filter to more clearly identify qualifying tax-exempt organizations.

- Completing a risk assessment on compliance issues related to the credit. The assessment identified risks involving refunds for tax-exempt entities, difficulties verifying employment tax return information for certain employers, and not using existing Math Error Authority (MEA).

- Considering the costs and benefits of MEA for the credit.[40] IRS officials identified three filters whose type of errors could be addressed with MEA. They noted that less than 1 percent of Forms 8941 tripped one or more of those filters,[41] which IRS officials said

---

[39]See GAO, *Tax Gap: Complexity and Taxpayer Compliance,* GAO-11-747T (Washington, D.C.: June 28, 2011).

[40]The Internal Revenue Code provides IRS with MEA to assess additional tax or otherwise correct tax return errors in limited circumstances when an adjustment is the result of mathematical or clerical errors on the return. In these cases, IRS can avoid costly audits and IRS is not required to provide taxpayers a right to appeal MEA assessments, although they may file a claim to ask IRS to reduce the assessment if they believe IRS erred. See 26 U.S.C. § 6213(b). Over the years, Congress has granted MEA for specific purposes and those purposes are listed in section 6213(g)(2).

[41]These three IRS filters are to check whether credit claims are consistent with eligibility requirements subject to computation criteria.

does not justify the costs to develop procedures to use MEA, if it were granted.[42]

Filters Check Some Eligibility Criteria, but Are Limited by Available Data

IRS developed 21 filters for Form 8941, some of which apply differently to SB/SE and TEGE taxpayers. The filters cover some of the eligibility requirements for the credit. Errors on about 3.5 percent (11,763) of Forms 8941 for tax year 2010 tripped 1 or more filters; almost half of those forms were from tax-exempt entities. According to IRS officials, the filter failure rate is consistent with other recent tax credits.

The filters do not cover all of the credit's requirements for several data-related reasons.[43] In one case, data are not included on Form 8941 but may be included on worksheets required to be retained by claimants (e.g., information on business owner family members or seasonal employees included in credit calculations); in another case, certain data are not transcribed (e.g., the credit amount for certain claimants). For other requirements, IRS officials stated that reasonable filters cannot easily be developed because of challenges with matching data.

Some Form 8941 filters also face limitations mainly because of problems with data or IRS's systems.

- Filters are mutually exclusive, meaning that filters on related requirements are viewed in isolation. However, according to IRS officials, IRS has ways to identify whether a form failed more than one filter, which IRS considers when identifying returns for potential examination.

- Some filters may mistakenly target eligible claimants because the filters rely on general thresholds in Form 8941 data or, in some cases, other IRS data (such as employee-level data) that are not exact matches to data on the Form 8941.

---

[42]We previously recommended that Congress should consider broadening IRS's ability to use MEA, with appropriate safeguards against misuse. See GAO, *Recovery Act: IRS Quickly Implemented Tax Provisions, but Reporting and Enforcement Improvements Are Needed,* GAO-10-349 (Washington, D.C.: Feb. 10, 2010).

[43]We do not describe the filters and the eligibility requirements not being covered in detail because of concerns about revealing IRS's compliance approach and criteria.

Data on Forms W-2 (employees' annual Wage and Tax Statement) could provide additional data for filters once the provision in PPACA is implemented that requires employers to report the cost—including both employer and employee contributions—of certain types of health insurance provided to an employee.[44] IRS officials said the data have limited use because, among other things, they would not provide details for determining whether an employer met the credit's requirements for health insurance; therefore, IRS officials will not pursue using the data at this time. Nevertheless, the data could be used in a filter to identify claimants who reported no health insurance contributions on Form W-2 and therefore may not be offering health insurance. In the absence of other documentation or third-party reporting on health insurance, using Form W-2 data in a filter could be a cost-effective, rough indicator of whether a claimant is paying employee health insurance premiums, without increasing taxpayer burden. However, IRS provided transition relief to employers that file fewer than 250 Forms W-2 per year, and issued guidance stating that these employers will not be required to report the data until further guidance is issued. As a result, it is unlikely that the data could be useful before 2014, the year when the credit will only be available to employers for any 2 consecutive years.

Examination Instructions Cover Most Eligibility Requirements, but Gaps Exist

After the filters are run, IRS creates lists of claims to consider for further examination. SB/SE wanted enough examination cases to spot check different filters and claims from different regions, to enable them to establish a field presence and to learn about compliance risks with the credit, according to an SB/SE official.[45] Examination staff in SB/SE and TEGE are to follow a set of instructions when doing examinations.[46]

SB/SE's examination instructions address all of the credit's requirements for small businesses to claim the credit except that they do not include

---

[44]See 26 U.S.C. § 6051(a)(14), which generally requires employers to report the aggregate cost of employer-sponsored coverage they provide for an employee on Form W-2.

[45]TEGE established two mandatory filters that if failed, automatically trigger an exam; only 16 forms tripped these two filters, as of December 31, 2011.

[46]Examiner instructions consist of several types of documents, such as worksheets and checklists on the credit's eligibility requirements; we also refer to these documents as examination "guidance."

specific instructions for examiners on determining eligibility of claimants with non-U.S. addresses. An employer located outside of the United States with a business or trade interest in the United States may claim the credit only if the employer pays premiums for coverage issued in and regulated by one of the states or the District of Columbia. Without a prompt in examination instructions, IRS examiners may overlook claimants that do not comply with the address requirements. An SB/SE official said IRS has no instructions for examiners to review claimants with non-U.S. addresses during an examination on the credit because potential compliance problems with businesses with non-U.S. addresses exist for other tax credits. This, however, was not IRS's approach for another general business tax issue relevant to the credit—whether claimants that carry back the credit to offset tax liabilities in previous years did so properly. Near the end of our work, SB/SE added guidance to one of its examination instruction documents to cover the carry back issue.

Instructions for TEGE examiners also address most of the eligibility requirements to claim the credits, but, like SB/SE's, TEGE examination instructions do not address how to review claimants with non-U.S. addresses.[47] Further, TEGE instructions for some of the credit's requirements have less detail compared to SB/SE's instructions. TEGE's instructions provide steps on how to determine if an employer's insurance premiums paid met "qualifying arrangement" and other criteria, but they provide less detail than SB/SE instructions. For example, SB/SE guidance instructs examiners to review health insurance policies and invoices to confirm premium payments, and to review other documentation to check whether the employer offers health benefits that are not eligible for the credit. TEGE instructions do not suggest these steps and also do not provide a prompt for examiners to ensure that insurance premiums paid on behalf of seasonal employees are included in calculations.

According to IRS officials, the TEGE examiners are trained specifically for doing examinations on the credit and therefore need less guidance than SB/SE examiners, who work on multiple issues simultaneously. However, TEGE examination documents contain detailed guidance in a workbook

---

[47]Tax-exempt entities with non-U.S. addresses must pay health insurance premiums for an employee's coverage issued in and regulated in one of the states or the District of Columbia.

format for these trained examiners on other credit requirements. Without detailed guidance for TEGE examiners that instructs them on how to examine health insurance documents, examiners may not consistently identify noncompliance, which could lead to erroneous credit refunds. This could particularly be the case as examining health insurance documents to check eligibility for this new credit has not been typical work for these examiners.

Examinations Under Way, but IRS Needs to Develop a Plan for Efficiently Analyzing Results on Credit Compliance

For tax year 2010, SB/SE plans to conduct over 1,500 examinations related to the credit, and TEGE anticipates about 1,000 examinations. An SB/SE official said the number of examinations is expected to provide initial compliance information and allow IRS to establish a compliance presence without committing too many resources initially. TEGE selected its number of examinations based on resource decisions, before tax year 2010 claims began. Neither SB/SE nor TEGE adjusted the number of examinations once actual claim numbers were known. As a result, the percentage of TEGE claims being examined is high, according to a TEGE official. Table 1 summarizes the status of IRS's examinations on the credit.

Table 1: Examination Actions for Form 8941 as of February 2012, for Tax Year 2010

Number of:	SB/SE[a]	TEGE	Total
Examinations initiated	500	570	1,070
Additional examinations anticipated	1,000	430	1,430
Closed examinations	119	88	207
Closed examinations resulting in a change to the credit amount	46	22	68

Sources: SB/SE and TEGE officials.

[a]For examinations, SB/SE does not distinguish between examinations on business or individual claimants.

IRS's database on examination results tracks the aggregate dollar amount of tax changes as a result of the examination but does not contain the reason a change is made. Consequently, IRS is not able to isolate and analyze examination results related to the credit versus other tax issues. This is particularly a problem for SB/SE examinations, which may cover issues other than the credit.[48] Instead, as initial examinations

---

[48]TEGE examinations will only cover the credit, according to IRS officials.

GAO-12-549 Small Employer Health Tax Credit

have closed, IRS officials said that management has spoken with examiners about findings related to the credit. This has been possible because of the relatively low initial volume of cases, but this approach may not be feasible as results accumulate. Therefore, it is not clear how IRS can efficiently analyze results to decide whether changes are necessary in how it examines the credit or how it educates small employers about how to comply with the credit's rules, and whether it committed too many or too few resources to examinations of the credit.

Furthermore, IRS does not have criteria for deciding whether the resources spent on examinations of the credit are appropriate, given the amount of errors found. IRS officials said that for future years they plan to select the number of credit examinations based on past results, identified compliance risks, and available resources. However, without criteria to assess the results in concert with these risks and resources, IRS is less able to ensure that examination resources target errors with the credit, rather than examining compliant claimants.

For example, early examination results (as of February 2012) show that 67 percent of the examinations completed were closed without changing the credit amount. Examinations without a change burden taxpayers and use IRS resources. We recognize that few of the planned examinations have been completed and the "no change" percentage could change. According to IRS officials, cases resulting in "no change" tend to be the first cases closed because they close more quickly than cases requiring a change. However, IRS is not using change rate information from prior tax credits to determine if examinations for the credit have a "high" no-change rate, which could be one indicator to help decide how many examination resources to apply to the credit. IRS officials said they do not plan to use data from examinations of other tax provisions to benchmark measures— such as the no-change rate or length of time an examination is open— because results would not be comparable.

A summary of examination results specific to the credit could also inform decisions about using additional compliance tools such as soft notices.[49] In the past, IRS has used soft notices to correct errors and collect funds

---

[49]A soft notice is a letter generated to taxpayers that IRS has identified possible errors on the taxpayer's form. The goal is to increase compliance at minimal costs by educating taxpayers for future compliance without doing an examination and minimizing the taxpayers' need to respond to the notice.

without initiating an examination.[50] A senior IRS official who is implementing the credit said IRS has not ruled out using soft notices, but examination results would need to identify an issue that would justify their use. He said soft notices are not effective for all taxpayers or situations. He said IRS would consider using soft notices if officials found a series of returns with mistakes from the same tax preparer or promoter of tax schemes. Furthermore, soft notices may necessitate follow-up, which would negate some of the advantages of the notices. If IRS analysis showed that examinations were not a cost-effective way to pursue certain errors made in claiming a credit, a soft notice may offer another approach to improving compliance with lower costs to IRS and less burden on claimants.

Data to Evaluate Many Questions about the Effects of the Credit Are Not Available

There are a variety of research questions that could be of interest to policymakers about the effects of the credit that cannot be evaluated with data currently available. Figure 5 shows how the credit may influence employer behavior and, ultimately, employees.

---

[50]For example, see GAO, *Advance Earned Income Tax Credit: Low Use and Small Dollars Paid Impede IRS's Efforts to Reduce High Noncompliance*, GAO-07-1110 (Washington, D.C.: Aug. 10, 2007), and *Tax Gap: IRS Could Do More to Promote Compliance by Third Parties with Miscellaneous Income Reporting Requirements*, GAO-09-238 (Washington, D.C.: Jan. 28, 2009).

Figure 5: Model of Potential Outcomes and Influential Factors for the Small Employer Health Insurance Tax Credit

Inputs/ investment	Outputs—who gets what	Potential outcomes/ impact
• Forfeited tax revenue • Implementation costs for IRS • Employer costs for purchasing insurance and claiming the credit	• Tax credit to certain small employers with low-wage employees that offer health insurance	**Small low wage employers claimants** • Begin offering health insurance, keep offering insurance or upgrade insurance plans • Savings on insurance premiums, possibly leading to re-inestment in the business or the business or organization

Employees of claimants
- Gain or maintain access to employer-sponsored health insurance
- Lower out-of-pocket costs for health care because of employer's ability to upgrade insurance plans
- Increased wages because of employers saving on insurance premiums

Potential influential factors

• General economic conditions • Labor market/ unemployment	• Effect of PPACA provisions on the insurance market, including exchanges • Other regulatory or tax policies affecting small employers	• Changes in eligibility requirements for the credit • Politics

Sources: GAO analysis and University of Wisconsin Extension Program Development and Evaluation model.

Note: Basic model structure is based on University of Wisconsin Extension Program Development and Evaluation model, as shown in GAO-12-208G. Content and relationships among variables are based on GAO analysis of interviews with subject matter specialists, and literature review.

To answer research questions about the credits potential outcomes shown in figure 5, the following are examples of data that might be needed:

- number of small, low-wage employers offering health insurance, before and after the credit was available;
- number of employees at small, low-wage employers, who have or could obtain health insurance through their employers; and
- amount of annual health insurance premium costs for small, low-wage employers before and after the credit.

None of these data are readily available or free of limitations, which complicates an evaluation. For example, the available data on employer-sponsored health insurance do not align with the credit's eligibility criteria, according to our interviews with subject matter specialists and our review of the data (see app. VI for a summary of the data sources), nor could we identify a data source that tracks when, and why, employers begin offering insurance. As a result of the limitations with all three types of data, it would be difficult to precisely measure changes in health insurance availability, offering, and costs because of the credit, without collecting additional data. Isolating influential factors—such as those shown in figure 5—that may contribute to the effects of the credit would also be a challenge in an evaluation.[51]

IRS officials said they will not collect data on credit claimants, outside of those collected on Form 8941. IRS's position on data collection for all provisions of the tax code is that it only collects data it needs to ensure compliance with the tax laws.[52]

Collecting additional data needed for policy evaluation would have costs, and the magnitude of those costs would depend on the type and amount of data needed, which depends on the research questions being asked. An additional consideration in thinking about the benefits and costs of additional data collection for policy evaluation purposes is the time limits on claiming the credit. The current version of the credit runs through the end of 2014.[53] Policymakers' conclusions about the questions to be answered by any evaluations of the credit's effects would determine the type of data that would need to be collected.

Conclusions

The Small Employer Health Insurance Tax Credit was intended to offer an incentive for small, low-wage employers to provide health insurance. However, utilization of the credit has been lower than expected, with the available evidence suggesting that the design of the credit is a large part of the reason why. While the credit could be redesigned, such changes

---

[51]For details on methods for identifying causation, including experiments and quasi-experiments, using comparison groups, see GAO, *Designing Evaluations: 2012 Revision*, GAO-12-208G (Washington, D.C.: January 2012). These designs are not feasible for the credit because it was implemented simultaneously across the country.

[52]See GAO, *Government Performance and Accountability: Tax Expenditures Represent a Substantial Federal Commitment and Need to Be Reexamined*, GAO-05-690 (Washington, D.C.: Sept. 23, 2005).

[53]Starting in 2014, eligible small employers can claim the credit for the 2 consecutive years beginning when the employer first offers employee health insurance from a state exchange.

GAO-12-549 Small Employer Health Tax Credit

come with trade-offs. Changing the credit to expand eligibility or make it more generous would increase the revenue loss to the federal government.

In administering the credit to ensure compliance, IRS employed a number of practices that were shown effective for other tax provisions or are consistent with IRS strategic objectives. Nevertheless, we identified several opportunities for IRS to either improve compliance or perhaps reduce the resources it is devoting to ensuring compliance. Without additional guidance for examiners on employers with non-U.S. addresses, there is a risk of improper credit claims being allowed. Without more systematic attention to early examination results, IRS could lock itself into devoting more scarce resources than needed to examinations.

Recommendations for Executive Action

To help ensure thoroughness and consistency of examinations on the credit, we recommend that the Commissioner of Internal Revenue take the following two actions:

1. Revise the SB/SE and TEGE examination instructions to include instructions for examiners on how to confirm eligibility for the credit for small employers with non-U.S. addresses.

2. Revise the TEGE examination guidance to include more detailed instructions for examiners on how to confirm that claimants properly calculated eligible health insurance premiums paid for purposes of the credit. The SB/SE examination instructions could serve as a model.

To help ensure that IRS uses its examination resources efficiently, we recommend that the Commissioner of Internal Revenue take the following two actions:

3. Document and analyze the results of examinations involving the credit to identify how much of those results are related to the credit versus other tax issues being examined, what errors are being made in claiming the credit, and when the examinations of the credit are worth the resource investment.

4. Related to the above analysis of examination results on the credit, identify the types of errors with the credit that could be addressed with alternative approaches, such as soft notices.

Agency Comments and Our Evaluation

In an April 30, 2012, letter responding to a draft of this report (which is reprinted in app. VII), the IRS Deputy Commissioner for Services and Enforcement provided comments on our findings and recommendations as well as information on additional agency efforts related to implementing the Small Employer Health Insurance Tax Credit in PPACA. IRS generally agreed with all four of our recommendations. Regarding our recommendation on examination instructions related to small employers with non-U.S. addresses, IRS stated that SB/SE will provide additional guidance in its instructions and that TEGE has added guidance to its instructions. On May 1, 2012, IRS provided a copy of the TEGE instructions, which we are reviewing. On our recommendation on revising TEGE's examination guidance, IRS's letter said that on April 13, 2012, TEGE implemented more detailed instructions in its examination guidance related to confirming proper calculations of eligible health insurance premiums paid for purposes of the credit. These instructions were also included in the TEGE document provided on May 1, 2012.

With regard to analyzing credit examination results to identify compliance issues specific to the credit, IRS said it regularly analyzes audit results to determine whether resources are expended efficiently, though its information systems do not currently capture adjustments by issue, such as this tax credit. IRS agreed to leverage existing information systems and, as appropriate, to allocate resources to manually analyze examination results. IRS said this will include, as feasible, identifying the types and amounts of errors related to the credit. We reiterate the benefit of documenting and analyzing the results of examinations involving the credit. If it does not do so, IRS will not have information for determining whether examinations of the credit are worth the resource investment.

Regarding our fourth recommendation on using examination results to determine whether alternative compliance approaches, such as soft notices, could help address errors with the credit, IRS agreed to continue to review its compliance efforts to determine whether soft notices would be appropriate.

As agreed with your offices, unless you publicly announce the contents of this report earlier, we plan no further distribution until 30 days from the report date. At that time, we will send copies to the Chairmen and Ranking Members of other Senate and House committees and subcommittees that have appropriation, authorization, and oversight responsibilities for IRS. We will also send copies to the Commissioner of Internal Revenue, the Secretary of the Treasury, the Chairman of the IRS

Oversight Board, and the Director of the Office of Management and Budget. In addition, the report will be available at no charge on the GAO website at http://www.gao.gov.

If you or your staff have any questions or about this report, please contact me at (202) 512-9110 or at whitej@gao.gov. Contact points for our Offices of Congressional Relations and Public Affairs may be found on the last page of this report. GAO staff who made key contributions to this report are listed in appendix VIII.

James R. White
Director, Tax Issues
Strategic Issues

Appendix I: Scope and Methodology

To assess the extent to which the Small Employer Health Insurance Tax Credit (referred to in this report as the credit) is being claimed, we obtained and analyzed Internal Revenue Service (IRS) data on the claims on Form 8941 for tax year 2010. We interviewed responsible IRS staff and examined background materials. IRS provided a report from the Form 8941 data and we reviewed the programming code that created that report. We corroborated the results of this IRS report with a Treasury Inspector General for Tax Administration (TIGTA) report published in November and found similarities.[1] The data were found to be sufficiently reliable for our purposes. We identified estimates of employers that were potentially eligible to claim the credit by reviewing reports and websites of government agencies, think tanks, and interest groups. When possible, we interviewed officials from the government agencies and business groups that developed estimates.

To identify any factors limiting credit claims, we interviewed groups representing employers, tax preparers and insurance brokers and to assess how these factors could be addressed, we analyzed our interview results as well as relevant documents. Specifically, we spoke with representatives of the National Federation of Independent Businesses, the National Council of Nonprofits, the Small Business Majority, the U.S. Chamber of Commerce, the American Institute of Certified Public Accountants, America's Health Insurance Plans, the National Society of Accountants, the National Association of Enrolled Agents, and the National Association of Health Underwriters. We worked with some of these groups to assemble discussion groups with tax preparers, health insurance brokers, and employers to discuss potential factors and ways to address them. Discussion groups were, for the most part, telephone conferences. We also spoke with insurance and tax preparation companies, specifically, BlueCross Blue Shield of Kansas City, Independent Health of New York, H&R Block's Tax Institute, and Jackson Hewitt Tax Service. We used qualitative analysis software to do a content analysis of the interviews and discussion group comments.

To provide additional support for discussion group and interview findings we reviewed documents and, where possible, we identified data from IRS, the 2010 Medical Expenditure Panel Survey, or the 2011 Kaiser

---

[1]TIGTA, *Affordable Care Act: Efforts to Implement the Small Business Health Care Tax Credit Were Mostly Successful, but Some Improvements Are Needed*, 2011-40-103 (Washington, D.C.: Sept. 19, 2011).

Family Foundation Health Benefits Survey. At IRS, we interviewed officials from the Small Business/Self-Employed Division (SB/SE), including officials in the Communications and Liaison Office; the Tax Exempt and Government Entities Division (TEGE); the Research and Analysis for Tax Administration division, and the Taxpayer Advocacy Service.

To assess how fully IRS is ensuring that the tax credit is correctly claimed by eligible employers, we reviewed IRS's compliance plan and filters and instructions for IRS staff conducting examinations, and compared these documents with compliance practices used for prior tax provisions and found in IRS strategic objectives.[2] We also highlighted any gaps between filters and examination instructions and the credit's eligibility rules. We reviewed the filter results for tax year 2010 claims and interviewed SB/SE and TEGE officials about compliance efforts.

To assess what would be needed to evaluate the effects of credit, we conducted a literature review and interviewed representatives of the forenamed groups and subject matter specialists from government, academia, research foundations and think tanks. We selected the specialists based primarily on our literature review and spoke with individuals at the University of Massachusetts, Boston; Massachusetts Institute of Technology; the Commonwealth Fund; the Urban Institute; the Kaiser Family Foundation; the American Enterprise Institute; the Employee Benefit Research Institute; the RAND Corporation; the Small Business Administration Office of Advocacy; and the Office of Tax Policy at the Department of the Treasury. We reviewed available data in commonly cited surveys with questions on employer health insurance, and identified how the questions and variables match to the eligibility criteria for the credit.

We conducted this performance audit from July 2011 through May 2012 in accordance with generally accepted government auditing standards. Those standards require that we plan and perform the audit to obtain sufficient, appropriate evidence to provide a reasonable basis for our findings and conclusions based on our audit objectives. We believe that

---

[2]For example, see GAO, *Tax Refunds: Enhanced Prefund Compliance Checks Could Yield Significant Benefits,* GAO-11-691T (Washington, D.C.: May 25, 2011).

the evidence obtained provides a reasonable basis for our findings and conclusions based on our audit objectives.

Appendix II: State Average Premiums for Small Group Markets for 2010 and 2011

The Small Employer Health Insurance Tax Credit is based on a percentage of the lesser of (1) the premiums paid by the eligible small employer for employees during the taxable year and (2) the amount of premiums the employer would have paid if each employee were enrolled in a plan with a premium equal to the average premium for the small group market in the state (or in an area in the state) in which the employer is offering health insurance. The Secretary of Health and Human Services determines whether separate average premiums will apply for areas within a state and also determines the average premium for a state or substate area. Table 2 shows the average premiums for the small group market in each state for tax years 2010 and 2011.

Table 2: State Average Premiums for Small Group Markets for 2010 and 2011

	2010		2011	
	Employee only (single plan)	Family plan	Employee only (single plan)	Family plan
Alabama	$4,441	$11,275	$4,778	$12,084
Alaska	6,204	13,723	6,729	14,701
Arizona	4,495	10,239	4,614	11,063
Arkansas	4,329	9,677	4,378	9,849
California	4,628	10,957	4,790	11,493
Colorado	4,972	11,437	5,007	12,258
Connecticut	5,419	13,484	5,640	14,096
Delaware	5,602	12,513	5,902	13,411
District of Columbia	5,355	12,823	5,721	14,024
Florida	5,161	12,453	5,218	12,550
Georgia	4,612	10,598	5,085	11,440
Hawaii	4,228	10,508	4,622	11,529
Idaho	4,215	9,365	4,379	10,066
Illinois	5,198	12,309	5,565	13,176
Indiana	4,775	11,222	5,262	12,097
Iowa	4,652	10,503	4,694	11,051
Kansas	4,603	11,462	4,693	11,909
Kentucky	4,287	10,434	4,456	10,560
Louisiana	4,829	11,074	5,143	11,911
Maine	5,215	11,887	5,261	12,255
Maryland	4,837	11,939	5,073	12,530
Massachusetts	5,700	14,138	5,900	15,262
Michigan	5,098	12,364	5,195	12,539

	2010		2011	
	Employee only (single plan)	**Family plan**	**Employee only (single plan)**	**Family plan**
Minnesota	4,704	11,938	5,048	12,790
Mississippi	4,533	10,501	4,787	10,860
Missouri	4,663	10,681	4,843	11,379
Montana	4,772	10,212	4,923	10,789
Nebraska	4,715	11,169	5,130	12,057
Nevada	4,553	10,297	4,781	10,836
New Hampshire	5,519	13,624	5,858	14,523
New Jersey	5,607	13,521	5,868	14,093
New Mexico	4,754	11,404	5,146	12,328
New York	5,442	12,867	5,589	13,631
North Carolina	4,920	11,583	5,136	11,949
North Dakota	4,469	10,506	4,545	11,328
Ohio	4,667	11,293	4,706	11,627
Oklahoma	4,838	11,002	4,922	11,200
Oregon	4,681	10,890	4,881	11,536
Pennsylvania	5,039	12,471	5,186	12,671
Rhode Island	5,887	13,786	5,956	14,553
South Carolina	4,899	11,780	5,036	11,780
South Dakota	4,497	11,483	4,733	11,589
Tennessee	4,611	10,369	4,744	11,035
Texas	5,140	11,972	5,172	12,432
Utah	4,238	10,935	4,532	11,346
Vermont	5,244	11,748	5,426	12,505
Virginia	4,890	11,338	5,060	12,213
Washington	4,543	10,725	4,776	11,151
West Virginia	4,986	11,611	5,356	12,724
Wisconsin	5,222	12,819	5,284	13,911
Wyoming	5,266	12,163	5,430	12,867

Source: Department of Health and Human Services and RS information.

Appendix III: Adjustments in Counting Total Small Employer Claims and Total Credit Amount Claims for Tax Year 2010

Internal Revenue Service (IRS) data for tax year 2010 show 335,600 total claims filed. This total must be adjusted to avoid counting the 110,800 S corporation and partnership claims that were passed through to 165,300 respective shareholders and partners who then filed their claims separately. Excluding the 165,300 shareholder and partner claims filed leaves 170,300 small employer claims filed. To capture the number of credit amounts claimed and avoid the amounts that were claimed by the S corporations and partnerships as well as their respective shareholders and partners, we excluded the 110,800 S corporation and partnership claims to arrive at 224,800 credit amounts claimed. (See fig. 6.)

Figure 6: Number of Credit Claims by Taxpayer Type, Tax Year 2010

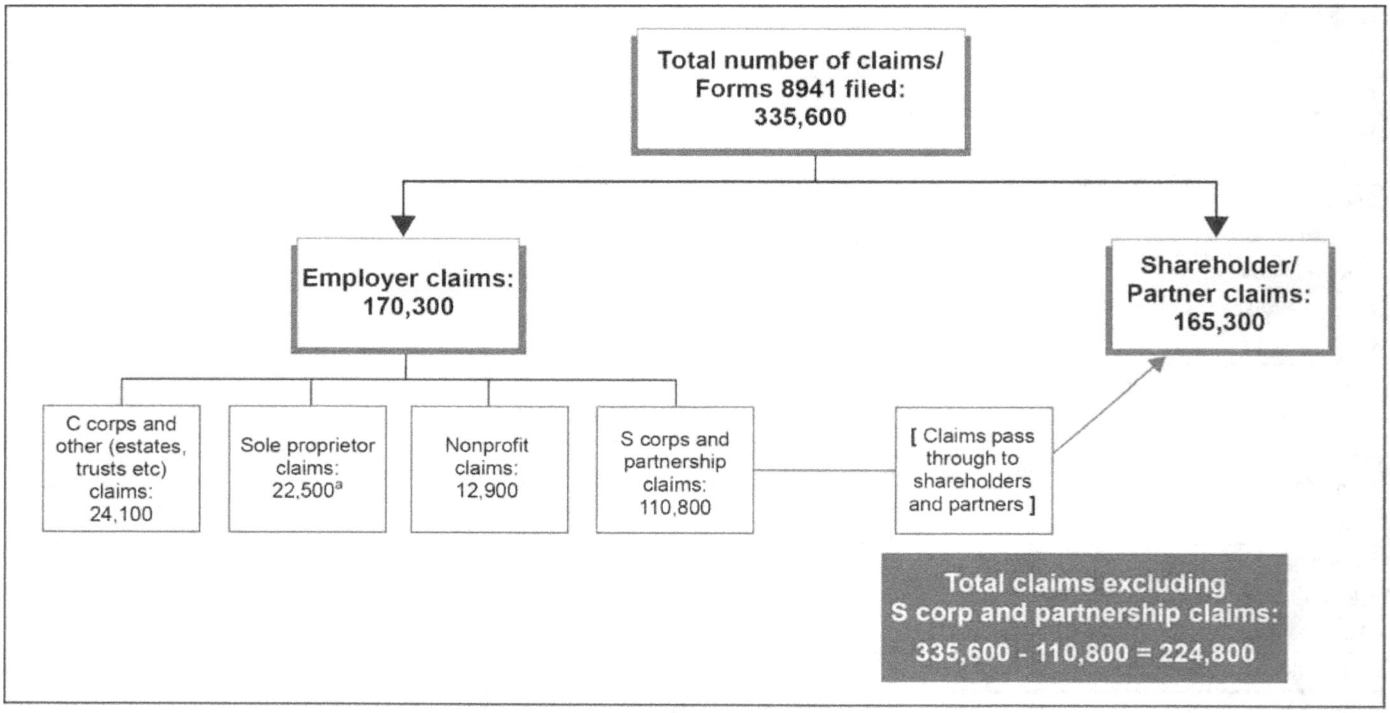

Source: GAO analysis of IRS data.

Note: Numbers rounded to the nearest hundred.

[a]Also included in this group are single member owners of disregarded limited liability corporations.

Appendix IV: Credit Claims by Employer Size and Wages Paid, Tax Year 2010

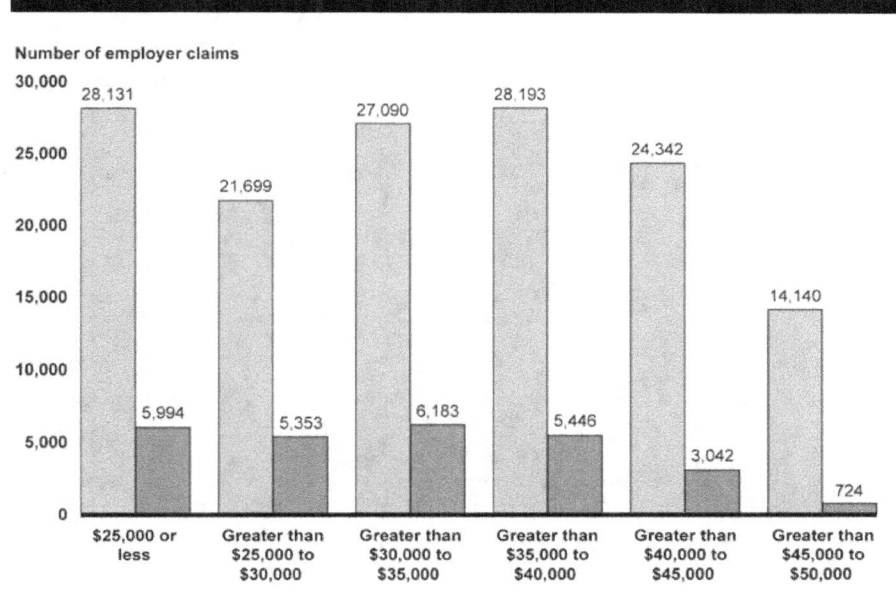

Number of employer claims

Average annual wages paid by claiming employers

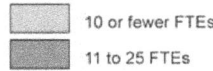
10 or fewer FTEs
11 to 25 FTEs

Source: GAO analysis of IRS data.

This appendix contains the noninteractive Form 8941 and worksheets, shown in figure 4 in the letter.

Form **8941**	**Credit for Small Employer Health Insurance Premiums**	OMB No. 1545-2198
Department of the Treasury Internal Revenue Service	▶ See separate instructions. ▶ Attach to your tax return.	20**10** Attachment Sequence No. **63**

Name(s) shown on return | Identifying number

1	Enter the number of individuals you employed during the tax year who are considered employees for purposes of this credit (see instructions)	**1**
2	Enter the number of full-time equivalent employees you had for the tax year (see instructions). If you entered 25 or more, skip lines 3 through 11 and enter -0- on line 12	**2**
3	Average annual wages you paid for the tax year (see instructions). If you entered $50,000 or more, skip lines 4 through 11 and enter -0- on line 12	**3**
4	Premiums you paid during the tax year for employees included on line 1 for health insurance coverage under a qualifying arrangement (see instructions)	**4**
5	Premiums you would have entered on line 4 if the total premium for each employee equaled the average premium for the small group market in which you offered health insurance coverage (see instructions)	**5**
6	Enter the **smaller** of line 4 or line 5	**6**
7	Multiply line 6 by the applicable percentage: • Tax-exempt small employers, multiply line 6 by 25% (.25) • All other small employers, multiply line 6 by 35% (.35)	**7**
8	If line 2 is 10 or less, enter the amount from line 7. Otherwise, see instructions	**8**
9	If line 3 is $25,000 or less, enter the amount from line 8. Otherwise, see instructions . . .	**9**
10	Enter the total amount of any state premium subsidies paid and any state tax credits available to you for premiums included on line 4 (see instructions)	**10**
11	Subtract line 10 from line 4. If zero or less, enter -0-	**11**
12	Enter the **smaller** of line 9 or line 11	**12**
13	If line 12 is zero, skip lines 13 and 14 and go to line 15. Otherwise, enter the number of employees included on line 1 for whom you paid premiums during the tax year for health insurance coverage under a qualifying arrangement (see instructions)	**13**
14	Enter the number of full-time equivalent employees you would have entered on line 2 if you only included employees included on line 13	**14**
15	Credit for small employer health insurance premiums from partnerships, S corporations, cooperatives, estates, and trusts (see instructions)	**15**
16	Add lines 12 and 15. Partnerships and S corporations, stop here and report this amount on Schedule K; all others, go to line 17	**16**
17	Credit for small employer health insurance premiums included on line 16 from passive activities (see instructions)	**17**
18	Subtract line 17 from line 16	**18**
19	Credit for small employer health insurance premiums allowed for 2010 from a passive activity (see instructions)	**19**
20	Carryback of the credit for small employer health insurance premiums from 2011	**20**
21	Add lines 18 through 20. Cooperatives, estates, and trusts, go to line 22. Tax-exempt small employers, skip lines 22 and 23 and go to line 24. All others, stop here and report this amount on Form 3800, line 29h	**21**
22	Amount allocated to patrons of the cooperative or beneficiaries of the estate or trust (see instructions)	**22**
23	Cooperatives, estates, and trusts, subtract line 22 from line 21. Stop here and report this amount on Form 3800, line 29h	**23**
24	Enter the amount you paid in 2010 for taxes considered payroll taxes for purposes of this credit (see instructions)	**24**
25	Tax-exempt small employers, enter the **smaller** of line 21 or line 24 here and on Form 990-T, line 44f	**25**

For Paperwork Reduction Act Notice, see separate instructions.   Cat. No. 37757S   Form **8941** (2010)

Source: IRS.

Worksheet 1. Information Needed To Complete Line 1 and Worksheets 2 and 3

If you need more rows, use a separate sheet and include the additional amounts in the totals below.

	(a) Individuals Considered Employees	(b) Employee Hours of Service	(c) Employee Wages Paid
1.			
2.			
3.			
4.			
5.			
6.			
7.			
8.			
9.			
10.			
11.			
12.			
13.			
14.			
15.			
16.			
17.			
18.			
19.			
20.			
21.			
22.			
23.			
24.			
25.			
Totals:			

Worksheet 2. Full-Time Equivalent Employees (FTEs)

1. Enter the total employee hours of service from Worksheet 1, column (b) . . . . 1. _____
2. Hours of service per FTE . . . . 2. ___2,080___
3. **Full-time equivalent employees.** Divide line 1 by line 2. If the result is not a whole number (0, 1, 2, etc.), generally round the result down to the next lowest whole number. However, if the result is less than one, enter 1. Report this amount on Form 8941, line 2 . . . . 3. _____

Worksheet 3. Average Annual Wages

1. Enter the total employee wages paid from Worksheet 1, column (c) . . . . 1. _____
2. Enter FTEs from Worksheet 2, line 3 . . . 2. _____
3. **Average annual wages.** Divide line 1 by line 2. If the result is not a multiple of $1,000 ($1,000, $2,000, $3,000, etc.), round the result down to the next lowest multiple of $1,000. Report this amount on Form 8941, line 3 . . . . 3. _____

Source: IRS.

Worksheet 4. Information Needed To Complete Lines 4 and 5 and Worksheet 7

If you need more rows, use a separate sheet and include the additional amounts in the totals below.

	(a) Enrolled Individuals Considered Employees	(b) Employer Premiums Paid	(c) Employer State Average Premiums	(d) Enrolled Employee Hours of Service
1.				
2.				
3.				
4.				
5.				
6.				
7.				
8.				
9.				
10.				
11.				
12.				
13.				
14.				
15.				
16.				
17.				
18.				
19.				
20.				
21.				
22.				
23.				
24.				
25.				
Totals:				

Worksheet 5. FTE Limitation

1. Enter the amount from Form 8941, line 7 .. 1. _____
2. Enter the amount from Form 8941, line 2 .... 2. _____
3. Subtract 10 from line 2 ...... 3. _____
4. Divide line 3 by 15. Enter the result as a decimal (rounded to at least 3 places) .... 4. _____
5. Multiply line 1 by line 4 .... 5. _____
6. Subtract line 5 from line 1. Report this amount on Form 8941, line 8 .... 6. _____

Worksheet 6. Average Annual Wage Limitation

1. Enter the amount from Form 8941, line 8 .... 1. _____
2. Enter the amount from Form 8941, line 7 .... 2. _____
3. Enter the amount from Form 8941, line 3 .... 3. _____
4. Subtract $25,000 from line 3 .... 4. _____
5. Divide line 4 by $25,000. Enter the result as a decimal (rounded to at least 3 places) .... 5. _____
6. Multiply line 2 by line 5 .... 6. _____
7. Subtract line 6 from line 1. Report this amount on Form 8941, line 9 .... 7. _____

Worksheet 7. FTEs Enrolled in Coverage

1. Enter the total enrolled employee hours of service from Worksheet 4, column (d) .. 1. _____
2. Hours of service per FTE .... 2. __2,080__
3. Divide line 1 by line 2. If the result is not a whole number (0, 1, 2, etc.), generally round the result down to the next lowest whole number. However, if the result is less than one, enter 1. Report this amount on Form 8941, line 14 .... 3. _____

Source: IRS.

Appendix VI: Publically Available Data on Small Employer Health Insurance

Through our literature review and interviews, we identified several commonly cited non-Internal Revenue Service data sources on employer health insurance. Each source has different variables related to the key eligibility requirements for the Small Employer Health Insurance Tax Credit. Table 3 summarizes each source, its basic methodology, and whether its data matches with these requirements for the credit. The table only considers data that are readily accessible in public-use data sets.

Table 3: Publically Available Data on Small Employer Health Insurance

	Employer Health Benefits Survey	Medical Expenditure Panel Survey (Insurance Component)	National Compensation Survey
Sources and methodology			
Organizations responsible for the survey	Kaiser Family Foundation and Health Research and Educational Trust	Department of Health and Human Services, Agency for Healthcare Research and Quality	Bureau of Labor Statistics
Frequency and contact method	Annual, conducted by phone	Annual, generally conducted by phone or mail	Annual, conducted by personal visits, mail, telephone, and e-mail
Unit of analysis, sample size and source	Employers—2,088 from Dun and Bradstreet and the Census of Governments	Employers[a]—38,409 private sector establishments from U.S. Census Bureau's Business Register	Employers;[b] 15,566 private industry establishments from state unemployment insurance reports
Response rate and most recent data, as of April 2012	Forth-seven percent in 2011	Eighty-three percent for private establishments in 2010	Fifty-six percent for private industry in 2011
Key eligibility requirement for the credit, and whether the source contains data			
Employer is a for-profit or tax-exempt entity	Yes	Yes	Yes[c]
Employer offers health insurance and pays at least 50 percent of premiums	Yes	Yes	Yes
Employer has fewer than 25 full-time equivalents (FTE)	No—number of employees	No—number of employees	No—number of employees, from 1 to 49, and number of full- and part-time employees
Average annual wages are less than $50,000 per FTE	No—percentage of full-time employees who make $23,000 or less per year	No—percentage of employees who earned wages in one of three categories[d]	No—wages are presented in five percentiles[e]

Source: GAO analysis of data sources.

[a]The Medical Expenditure Panel Survey's Insurance Component sample is drawn at the establishment level; an establishment is a particular workplace or location.

[b]The National Compensation Survey sample is drawn at the establishment level; an establishment is a single economic unit that engages in one, or primarily one, type of economic activity. It is usually a single physical location.

[c]Statistical models used by the National Compensation Survey are able to control for profit/non-profit status.

[d]The annual wage categories are about (1) $23,920 or less, (2)$23,920 to $54,080, and (3) $54,080 or more.

[e]Wage data are presented in percentile categories in the published data. The annual wage categories, for private industry workers, are about: (1) 10th percentile makes $17,160 or less, (2) 25th percentile makes $22,235 or less, (3) 50th percentile makes $33,009 or less, (4) 75th percentile makes $51,605 or less, and (5) the 90th percentile makes $78,811 or less.

Appendix VII: Comments from the Internal Revenue Service

DEPARTMENT OF THE TREASURY
INTERNAL REVENUE SERVICE
WASHINGTON, D.C. 20224

DEPUTY COMMISSIONER

April 30, 2012

Mr. James R. White
Director, Tax Issues
Strategic Issues Team
United States Government Accountability Office
Washington, DC 20548

Dear Mr. White:

Thank you for the opportunity to review your draft report entitled, "Small Employer Health Tax Credit: Factors Contributing to Low Use and Complexity (GAO-12-549, Job Code 450922). As your report notes, the IRS conducted significant outreach to ensure that eligible small businesses are aware of the credit, and have the information that they need to claim it.

With respect to your specific recommendations, the IRS agrees that more detailed instructions to examiners and more detailed data about examination results would be helpful improvements to our program. The enclosed response addresses each recommendation separately.

If you have questions, please contact me, or a member of your staff may contact Faris Fink, Commissioner, Small Business/Self-Employed Division at (202) 622-0600.

Sincerely,

Steven T. Miller
Deputy Commissioner for Services and
Enforcement

Enclosure

**GAO Recommendations and IRS Responses to GAO Draft Report
Small Employer Health Tax Credit: Factors Contributing to Low Use and Complexity
GAO-12-549**

Recommendation: Revise the SB/SE and TEGE examination instructions to include instructions for examiners on how to confirm eligibility for the credit for small employers with a non-U.S. address.

Comments: We agree with this recommendation. Although a foreign address does not necessarily reflect ineligibility for the credit, we agree that when a foreign address is listed, the examiner should take special care to ensure that the requirements for the credit are satisfied. SB/SE instructions and a current job aide explain that eligibility for the credit requires that health care premiums are paid to a U.S. regulated insurance carrier and that the credit is applied to a U.S. federal tax liability. SB/SE will supplement existing guidance to highlight this area and provide additional information for auditing this issue. TEGE has also developed and implemented additional examination instructions for examiners on how to confirm eligibility for the credit for small employers with a non-U.S. address. These additional instructions for examiners are based upon published guidance.

Recommendation: Revise the TEGE examination guidance to include more detailed instructions for examiners on how to confirm that claimants properly calculated eligible health insurance premiums paid, for purposes of the credit. The SB/SE examination instructions could serve as a model.

Comments: We agree with this recommendation. TEGE has revised its written examination guidance to include more detailed instructions for examiners on how to confirm that claimants properly calculated eligible health insurance premiums paid, for purposes of the credit. These revisions were based upon SB/SE examination instructions and were implemented on April 13, 2012.

Recommendation: Document and analyze the results of examinations involving the credit to identify how much of those results are related to the credit versus other tax issues being examined, what errors are being made in claiming the credit, and when the examinations of the credit are worth the resource investment.

Comments: We agree with this recommendation. We regularly analyze audit results to determine whether resources are being expended efficiently. Currently, our information systems do not capture adjustments by issue. However, we will leverage existing information systems and, as appropriate, allocate resources to manually analyze examination results to optimize our compliance efforts. This will include, as feasible,

2

identifying what errors taxpayers are making in claiming the credit and how much of the examination results relate to the tax credit as opposed to other tax issues.

Recommendation: Related to the above analysis of examination results on the credit, identify the types of errors with the credit that could be addressed with alternative approaches, such as soft notices.

Comments: As noted above, the Service continuously strives to improve its compliance efforts. It uses all tools at its disposal—including soft notices—to promote compliance with the least burden to the taxpayer and the Service. We will continue to review our compliance efforts to determine whether the use of soft notices would be appropriate.

Appendix VIII: GAO Contact and Staff Acknowledgments

GAO Contact	James R. White, (202) 512-9110 or whitej@gao.gov
Staff Acknowledgments	In addition to the contact named above, Thomas Short, Assistant Director; Susan Baker; Amy Bowser; Ellen Grady; George Guttman; Donna Miller, Ruben Montes de Oca, Edward Nannenhorn; Robert Gebhart; Crystal Robinson; Cynthia Saunders; and Lindsay Swenson made key contributions to this report.

GAO's Mission	The Government Accountability Office, the audit, evaluation, and investigative arm of Congress, exists to support Congress in meeting its constitutional responsibilities and to help improve the performance and accountability of the federal government for the American people. GAO examines the use of public funds; evaluates federal programs and policies; and provides analyses, recommendations, and other assistance to help Congress make informed oversight, policy, and funding decisions. GAO's commitment to good government is reflected in its core values of accountability, integrity, and reliability.
Obtaining Copies of GAO Reports and Testimony	The fastest and easiest way to obtain copies of GAO documents at no cost is through GAO's website (www.gao.gov). Each weekday afternoon, GAO posts on its website newly released reports, testimony, and correspondence. To have GAO e-mail you a list of newly posted products, go to www.gao.gov and select "E-mail Updates."
Order by Phone	The price of each GAO publication reflects GAO's actual cost of production and distribution and depends on the number of pages in the publication and whether the publication is printed in color or black and white. Pricing and ordering information is posted on GAO's website, http://www.gao.gov/ordering.htm. Place orders by calling (202) 512-6000, toll free (866) 801-7077, or TDD (202) 512-2537. Orders may be paid for using American Express, Discover Card, MasterCard, Visa, check, or money order. Call for additional information.
Connect with GAO	Connect with GAO on Facebook, Flickr, Twitter, and YouTube. Subscribe to our RSS Feeds or E-mail Updates. Listen to our Podcasts. Visit GAO on the web at www.gao.gov.
To Report Fraud, Waste, and Abuse in Federal Programs	Contact: Website: www.gao.gov/fraudnet/fraudnet.htm E-mail: fraudnet@gao.gov Automated answering system: (800) 424-5454 or (202) 512-7470
Congressional Relations	Katherine Siggerud, Managing Director, siggerudk@gao.gov, (202) 512-4400, U.S. Government Accountability Office, 441 G Street NW, Room 7125, Washington, DC 20548
Public Affairs	Chuck Young, Managing Director, youngc1@gao.gov, (202) 512-4800 U.S. Government Accountability Office, 441 G Street NW, Room 7149 Washington, DC 20548